ॐ

DATE: _____

FROM: _____

TO: _____

MESSAGE: _____

_____

First edition

2   4   6   8   10   9   7   5   3   1

Library of Congress Catalog Card Number: 99-61674
ISBN 0-7892-0600-5

❦ MESSAGES OF FRIENDSHIP ❦

I Like You Just the Way You Are

Text by Helmut Walch

Photography by Andrew Cowin

ABBEVILLE PRESS PUBLISHERS

NEW YORK   LONDON   PARIS

I'm grateful for all that we've shared together. In your own special way, you've made so many of our hours together shine.

❧

Whether it's wrangling wild horses, planting a whole forest, traveling to the farthest reaches—whatever springs to your mind, wherever your thoughts take you—I'm with you. Because, because . . . well, there are lots of reasons.

Like a rock in a brook, you are a steadfast friend; like a shepherd with his flock— you're always there when a friend needs you. It feels good to rely on you; being able to count on you brings peace of mind.

Faultless, flawless, absolutely perfect? No, you aren't really—and you shouldn't be. It wouldn't suit you in the least. Your little weaknesses make you lovable. Stay just the way you are!

Friendship can't be bought or traded. Friendships mean work and nurturing. That is something you understand and practice.

❧

You're not silent as a statue.

But when you need to, you know how to keep a secret,

and a friend can count on you to be discreet.

❧

All friendships have their boundaries. We all have our private corners and niches that no one else should peer into. You're always respectful of my privacy.

$\mathcal{L}$et me say it once again: your eagerness to help goes both ways. I'm just as happy to stand by you as you are to stand by me.

A candid word at the right moment—not everyone can do it; not everyone has the courage. I value the moments when you are forthright with me—it is a mark of your sincerity.

❧

If it flatters you—so what?

I'm so proud of you, proud to count myself among your friends, proud to be close to you.

☙

You are such as strong person that a friend can come to you with his worries and you're never fazed by this aspect of friendship. I don't know if it's really as easy for you as you make it look—for this, I thank you.

❧

Did I say before that you're not without faults? Well, fine—who can claim to be without faults? In any case, not I. Your tolerance alone makes being with you easy.

In the warmest way, you give one the feeling of being needed. You awaken my sense of community and help me realize I can do things for others—and that's what's important in life.

There are things one doesn't need to possess; it's enough just to know they're there— that's all you need for peace of mind. That's how it is with you when it comes to consolation. I know that in my time of need, you'll be there for me.

❦

Over time, we all change; it's inevitable. It's true for you just as it is for me. But as a friend you've remained constant, and that makes me very happy.

You're not without your highs and lows, but you also know the art of balance and consideration. Your steadiness does me good and is there in all your friendships.

Our friendship calls to mind a port, a place of safe harbor, a place where one can prepare for new unknown adventures, a place of refuge and shelter.

I often have to smile at the way we communicate without uttering a word, not out of nervousness or having nothing to say, but because we are so harmonious. A little body language, a few gestures —that's all it takes and we understand each other.

You are willing to cross the line, and that is one of your special qualities as a friend. Your acceptance and respect of other viewpoints is a sign of your tolerance and wisdom.

Many are the times when you're a nose ahead of me; there are certain things that you're better at. Still, you never show the slightest doubt that we are equals, and that is a sign of true friendship.